S0-DQY-622

How to Grow
a Hundred Dollars

SANTA MARIA SCHOOL DISTRICT

Number_____118826

Santa Barbara County, California

How to Grow a Hundred Dollars

Elizabeth James and Carol Barkin

Illustrated by **Joel Schick**

Lothrop, Lee & Shepard Company
A Division of William Morrow & Company, Inc.
New York

For EDNA BARTH
with thanks

Copyright © 1979 by Elizabeth James and Carol Barkin
All rights reserved. No part of this book may be reproduced or utilized in any form or by any means, electronic or mechanical, including photocopying, recording or by any information storage and retrieval system, without permission in writing from the Publisher. Inquiries should be addressed to Lothrop, Lee & Shepard Company, 105 Madison Ave., New York, N. Y. 10016.
Printed in the United States of America.
First Edition   1 2 3 4 5 6 7 8 9 10

Library of Congress Cataloging in Publication Data

James, Elizabeth.
  How to grow a hundred dollars.

  SUMMARY: As she starts her own terrarium business, Amy is introduced to such basic economic principles as costs and inflation, profit and loss, interest and loans, advertising and attracting new investors, and eventual liquidation at a profit.
  1. Business—Juvenile literature. 2. Economics—Juvenile literature. [1. Business. 2. Economics] I. Barkin, Carol, joint author. II. Schick, Joel. III. Title.
HF5386.J347   658.4   78-31855
ISBN 0-688-41894-5   ISBN 0-688-51894-X lib. bdg.

Contents

1
Amy's Capital Idea

Amy Jackson looked around the dinner table at her family. "Gee," she said, "I've been thinking about that camping trip at the end of the summer. I sure wish I could go."

Her brother Danny helped himself to another slice of cake. "But Amy, that trip costs a hundred dollars. Where are you going to get that much money?"

"I don't know," Amy said. "Do you have any ideas?"

"GEE," SHE SAID, "I'VE BEEN THINKING ABOUT THAT CAMPING TRIP AT THE END OF THE SUMMER!"

Danny thought for a while. "How about making bird-houses like the one you made last summer? People would buy those."

"Great idea!" Amy said eagerly. "There's lots of scrap lumber in the basement. I'll go see if there's any paint left over."

Amy's Capital Idea

Amy clattered down the stairs, but in a few moments she was back, looking dejected. "I just remembered," she said. "It took me almost all summer to make that birdhouse. I'll never make enough money that way."

Danny said, "I see what you mean. But how about that hand-painted scarf you made? That didn't take any time at all."

"Oh, Danny, no one's wearing those anymore. There's no demand—I couldn't even give them away! But wait—Suzie asked me to make her a necklace like this one. I could make a lot of them. Do you think I'd find many buyers?"

Danny laughed. "Sure! I'd even buy one for Ann. But don't you remember? You spent your whole allowance on beads and wire to make that necklace. How much profit could you make after you paid for the raw materials?

"Oh yeah," sighed Amy. "I guess that won't work either. I'd have to charge too much and no one could afford them."

Standing up, Danny said, "Well, I've got to go meet Ann at the bowling alley. Keep thinking—I know you'll come up with something."

The goal of Amy's business venture (or any other) is

to end up with more money than she started with. This increase in money is called a profit. But of course, all the money received by a business is not profit. Some of the money must be used to pay the expenses of running the business and making the product. After all these expenses are paid, the money that is left over is the profit.

How can Amy decide what kind of business to start? She needs to produce something that other people want to buy. If she produces a large supply of things nobody wants, she won't be able to sell them for very much money; this means her profit will be very small. So Amy has to make sure there is a demand for whatever she decides to sell.

On her way to the library to look for a book on how to make money, Amy passed the pet store. Dozens of empty glass fishbowls were stacked everywhere. "Those are just like the bowl I used to make Mom's terrarium," Amy said to herself. "I wonder if I could make more terrariums and sell them?"

She went inside and found the owner, Mr. Buckley, sweeping up broken glass. "That's the third one I've broken today!" he exclaimed. "There's no room to turn around in this shop!"

"THAT'S THE THIRD ONE I'VE BROKEN TODAY!" HE EXCLAIMED.

"What are you going to do with all these fishbowls?" asked Amy.

"I don't know!" Mr. Buckley answered crossly. "I ordered them for the annual town picnic, but they decided not to have the ping-pong toss this year. Now I'm stuck with them!"

"How much are you selling them for?" Amy asked.
"You can have them for what I paid for them—a quarter apiece. Do you want some?" he asked eagerly.

"Maybe," Amy replied. Thinking furiously, she ran out of the store and all the way home.

At home Amy pulled out a scratch pad and a pencil. "Let's see," she said to herself, "I bet I could sell a whole lot of terrariums because all of Mom's friends thought the one I made for her was great. How much should I charge?" She thought a moment. "The florist sells terrariums just a little bigger for $5. If I sell mine for $3 apiece, that will be a bargain. If I sell 50 terrariums, I'll make $150. I'd better figure out how much these terrariums will cost to make."

50 fishbowls @ $.25	$12.50
potting soil, charcoal & vermiculite	$ 5.00
plants for 50 terrariums	$10.00
total costs	$27.50

income from 50 terrariums @ $3	$150.00
less costs	− 27.50
profit	$122.50

Amy was delighted with her calculations. "I'll have

extra money after I pay for the camping trip," she thought happily. But before investing in 50 fishbowls, Amy decided to find out how much demand there was for her terrariums.

Amy spent the afternoon going around her block and by the end of the day she had found eight customers. That night she explained her problem to Danny. "Eight sales in one afternoon is pretty good," she told him, "but I've already covered our whole neighborhood. How am I going to find more customers?"

"Why don't you ask Mr. Buckley if you can use a corner of his store?" Danny suggested.

"He doesn't have any room. That's why he's selling the fishbowls so cheaply," Amy replied.

Danny had run out of ideas, but suddenly Amy exclaimed, "I'll go to the Saturday swap meet! People sell all kinds of things there!"

"Good idea," said Danny. "You'd better get busy making your terrariums—you'll have to have them with you to sell."

The next days were busy ones for Amy. She wanted her terrariums to be gorgeous and she spent a lot of time planning what plants to use. Suddenly she realized she only had $15 in her money jar. She couldn't possibly buy all the bowls and plants and soil she needed for

50 terrariums with $15; her calculations had shown that she needed $27.50. "I guess I'll just buy half the stuff and make 25 terrariums first," she decided. "I forgot that I had to make the terrariums before I could sell them."

Any kind of business needs money to start with. This money is called capital. As Amy found out, the raw materials must be bought before the finished products can be made and sold. Amy had a total of $15 capital to invest in her business. When she spent $13.75 for raw materials, she invested almost all of her capital. This meant that until she made her first terrarium and sold it, she had only $1.25.

After Amy had enough materials for 25 terrariums, she quickly made the eight terrariums her neighbors had ordered. When she had delivered them, she had $24 from her sales to add to the $1.25. She was feeling pretty rich.

"This is great," Amy said to herself as she worked harder than ever getting terrariums ready for the swap meet. By Saturday she had 12 terrariums all finished.

"Hey, Amy, they look terrific," said Danny. "You'll probably make a lot of money."

Amy was busy packing the terrariums in her wagon. "I hope so," she replied. "But I need some help getting them over to the swap meet. Will you take the back end of the wagon?"

"Sure," he said. "But it'll cost you a quarter. Labor isn't free, you know."

When Amy and Danny got to the swap meet, they chose a good spot and began unpacking the wagon.

"WILL YOU TAKE THE BACK END OF THE WAGON?"

Amy was putting up her sign

AMY'S TERRARIUMS
ONLY $3.00

when the manager of the swap meet came up.

"Do you have a permit?" he asked Amy.

"No," answered Amy in surprise. "I didn't know I needed one."

"Oh, yes," the manager said. "It costs $2.25 but it's good for the whole summer."

As he walked away, Amy said to Danny, "I'll have to refigure my expenses when I get home. Here's your 25¢, Danny."

"Thanks," said Danny as he started to leave. "And good luck."

Amy smiled and turned to greet her first customer.

As the afternoon wore on, Amy sold six, then seven, then nine of her terrariums. She was feeling happy but tired when she stepped backward and suddenly heard a crash. One of the three remaining terrariums had smashed to the ground!

"Oh, no!" Amy cried as she stared at the mess. Even the plants were broken beyond repair.

When Amy got home, she got out her business record

sheet and began to enter the day's expenses and sales.

Amy's Terrariums Business Record Sheet

ORIGINAL CAPITAL		$15.00
EXPENSES		
25 fishbowls	$ 6.25	
soil, etc.	2.50	
plants	5.00	
	$13.75	−13.75
		$ 1.25
SALES 8 × $3.00 = $24.00		+24.00
		$25.25
EXPENSES		
labor	$ .25	
permit	2.25	
	$ 2.50	− 2.50
		$22.75
SALES 11 × $3.00 = $33.00		+33.00
		$55.75

Any business has other kinds of expenses besides the cost of the raw materials. The owner may have to pay rent for a factory or store and he probably also must pay for electricity, telephone, and whatever else is needed to keep his plant running. Amy didn't have to pay for the things she had for free at home such as telephone and electricity. In fact, she didn't have any operating expenses for her "factory." But she did have to pay "rent" for her shop when she had to pay a permit fee for her place at the swap meet.

Labor is a big expense for any business. A person who works for a business is selling service instead of selling goods. The owner of the business pays for the time and skills of his workers. Just as the owner must spend capital to buy raw materials, he must pay for the labor to produce his goods. Amy made all her terrariums herself, so she didn't have to pay anyone else to do this work. But when Danny helped her take the terrariums to the swap meet, she had to pay him for his labor. And to sell all 50 of her terrariums, she'd probably have to pay him for three more trips to the swap meet.

On another piece of paper Amy kept her calculations on how much money she would make from her terrarium business. When she started, she had figured she would make $122.50 profit from 50 terrariums. Now she had to revise this estimate. Her new estimated profit sheet looked like this:

ESTIMATED INCOME

        50 terrariums @ $3.00 $150.00

ESTIMATED EXPENSES

raw materials	$13.75 × 2 =	$27.50
labor	$.25 × 4 =	1.00
permit		2.25
		$30.75	− 30.75
			$119.25
Loss of 1 terrarium		$ 3.00	− 3.00
		Estimated Profit	$116.25

What other kinds of costs does a business have? Like Amy, most business owners sometimes have damaged goods that cannot be sold. The money they expected to receive for these goods must be counted as a loss. Amy's finished product was a $3.00 terrarium, not just an empty fishbowl and some plants and a pile of dirt. When the finished terrarium was broken, she lost a $3.00 sale.

You may have already figured out that if Amy had broken all of the 20 terrariums she made, her business loss would have been $60.00. This is much more money than she had actually spent on business expenses. But Amy's time and labor are worth money too—the selling

21

price of her terrariums must repay her for the work as well as the capital she has invested.

Danny peered over Amy's shoulder at her calculations. "Wow, you're doing really well," he said. "You'll be able to go on that camping trip after all."

"I hope so," Amy replied, "but I'll have to be careful not to break anything else!"

2
Green Thumb
Greenbacks

Just then the doorbell rang. It was Mr. Jeffreys from across the street. He told Amy that the terrarium he had bought from her was doing fine. Then he said, "I was wondering if you'd like to do some gardening work for me. I'll pay you $2.00 for an afternoon's work."

"Thanks, Mr. Jeffreys," said Amy, "but I'm too busy right now with my terrarium business."

"Okay," Mr. Jeffreys said cheerfully. "Hope your business is a big success—I'll tell my friends about it."

As Mr. Jeffreys left, Danny said to Amy, "What's the matter with you? You could have earned some extra money."

"But I can make more money with my terrariums. I've figured it out—look."

Expenses for 25 terrariums:	$16.25
Expenses for each terrarium:	
($16.25 divided by 25)	$.65
Profit per terrarium:	
($3.00 minus .65)	$2.35

"Even if I only made one terrarium in an afternoon, I'd earn more money for my time than I'd make gardening. And some days I can almost finish two terrariums," explained Amy.

"I guess you're right," Danny said in surprise.

Amy has discovered that the time she spends working is worth money. But it may not always be worth the same amount. If she didn't have her terrarium business, she might be happy to get $2.00 for an afternoon's work. On the other hand, if someone offers her $5.00 for an afternoon of running errands, she might decide to give up her terrariums for that day. The time anyone spends working is worth whatever an employer is willing to pay for it. Of course, money isn't the only thing that matters in choosing a job. But since Amy's goal is to make enough money for her camping trip, she has to choose the work that pays her the most money for her time.

THE TIME ANYONE SPENDS WORKING IS WORTH WHATEVER AN EMPLOYER IS WILLING TO PAY FOR IT.

Amy carefully patted the last plant in place. "I've used up all my raw materials," she told Danny. "I have to buy more fishbowls and soil and plants so I'll have more terrariums for the next swap meet."

"How are you going to pay for them?" asked Danny.

"I have plenty of money from the sales I've already made," replied Amy.

Danny looked surprised. "But I thought that money was for your camping trip."

"It is," said Amy. "But I have to spend some of it in order to make more."

What Amy is doing is reinvesting. She is using some of her profits to keep her business going. You can easily see that in any business, part of the profit must be used to pay for more raw materials and labor in order to keep the business running. Without this reinvestment, the business would simply shut down when all the raw materials were used up. Since Amy feels sure she can sell more of her terrariums, she wants to keep her business going.

When Amy came back with a new supply of raw materials, she decided to bring her business record sheet up to date.

Amy's Terrariums Business Record Sheet

ORIGINAL CAPITAL		$15.00
EXPENSES		
fishbowls	$ 6.25	
soil, etc.	2.50	
plants	5.00	
	$13.75	−13.75
		$ 1.25
SALES 8 × $3.00 = $24.00		+24.00
		$25.25
EXPENSES		
labor	$ .25	
permit	2.25	
	$2.50	− 2.50
		$22.75
SALES 11 × $3.00 = $33.00		+33.00
		$55.75
EXPENSES		
25 fishbowls	$ 6.25	
soil	2.50	
plants	5.00	
	$13.75	−13.75
		$42.00

"That looks good on paper," Amy said. She emptied her money jar onto her bed. "Let's see if I really have as much money as these calculations say I do!"

While Amy was counting her money, her friend Joan called. Amy told her how well the terrarium business was doing. "I've got $42.00 right here in my money jar!"

"That's great," said Joan. "But the money shouldn't be in your money jar—it should be in the savings bank. Then you'll have even more money."

"How can that be?" asked Amy.

When you keep your money in a savings account, the savings bank adds a little money to the amount you have put in. This extra money is called interest. The interest you receive is a percentage of the amount of money in your account.

It may seem strange that the bank pays you for keeping your money safe—it may seem that you should pay the bank for this service. But banks are in the business of borrowing and lending money. When you deposit money in a savings account, you are really lending your money to the bank. The bank in turn lends your money to other people and businesses.

People who borrow money from the bank must pay

THE BANK IN TURN LENDS YOUR MONEY
TO OTHER PEOPLE AND BUSINESSES.

interest on the amount they borrow. This interest is the fee people pay to "rent" money from the bank. The interest rate paid by a borrower is a higher percentage than the interest the bank pays its depositors. For example, a bank may pay 5% interest to savings account depositors and it may charge 9% interest to people who borrow money.

29

How to Grow a Hundred Dollars

$$\begin{array}{r} \$109 \\ -105 \\ \hline \$\ \ 4 \end{array}$$

The difference between the two interest rates is kept by the bank. The bank runs its business and makes its profit from this money.

Naturally, a bank has much more than $100 to lend. One important service a bank provides is to pool the money of many small depositors and make it available for loans to the community it serves.

The interest rates that a bank pays and receives are regulated by the government. All banks must offer the same percentage of interest for the same kind of account. But you can choose from several different types of savings accounts which pay different rates of interest. The bank pays a higher rate of interest if you promise to leave your money in your account for a certain amount of time. This is because the bank then knows that your savings will be available for loans.

Amy liked the idea of letting her money make more money while she was making more terrariums. When she got to the savings bank, she saw a list of all the different kinds of accounts and their rates of interest.

"I can't keep all my savings in the bank for a very long time," she thought. "I'll need to take a lot of money out to pay for my camping trip."

Amy decided to put her money into a regular savings account. She received a bankbook showing the amount of her first deposit.

AMY WALKED OVER TO ONE OF THE TELLERS TO OPEN A REGULAR SAVINGS ACCOUNT.

How to Grow a Hundred Dollars

"Every time you want to put money into your account or take it out, be sure to bring this bankbook," the teller said to Amy. "That way you'll have an accurate record of the money in your account."

"Thanks," said Amy. "I hope I'll be able to deposit more money soon so I can earn more interest."

3
Amy Floats a Loan

A week before the camping trip, Amy still didn't have the $100 she needed. Her terrariums had been a successful product, but she had had some other problems. One Saturday she was sick and another Saturday the swap meet was rained out, so she had only managed to sell 14 more terrariums. Her business record sheet looked like this:

How to Grow a Hundred Dollars

Amy's Terrariums Business Record Sheet

ORIGINAL CAPITAL		$15.00
EXPENSES		
fishbowls (25)	$ 6.25	
soil, etc.	2.50	
plants	5.00	
	$13.75	−13.75
		$ 1.25
SALES 8 × $3.00 = $24.00		+24.00
		$25.25
EXPENSES		
labor	$ .25	
permit	2.25	
	$2.50	− 2.50
		$22.75
SALES 11 × $3.00 = $33.00		+33.00
		$55.75
EXPENSES		
fishbowls (25)	$ 6.75	
soil, etc.	2.50	
plants	5.00	
	$13.75	−13.75
		$42.00
SALES 10 × $3.00 = $30.00		+30.00
		$72.00

$72.00

EXPENSES
    labor $ .25   − .25
                                           $71.75

SALES $4 \times \$3.00 = \$12.00$ +12.00
                                           $83.75

EXPENSES
    labor $ .25   − .25
                                           $83.50

And her savings account had earned less than $1.00 in interest, which didn't help much.

Amy needed to borrow some money to pay for the camping trip. She wanted to keep her savings account open, so she withdrew $80.00. She decided to ask her parents for a loan of $35.00—$20.00 for the rest of the trip fee and $15 for spending money.

When Amy's mother looked at Amy's business record sheet, she said, "Looks as if you have a profitable business. I'm sure you'll be able to repay the loan with future sales."

"I have 16 terrariums ready to sell when I come back," Amy said. "You'll get your money back pretty quickly. And, of course, I'll pay interest on the loan."

"That sounds good," said Mom, "but we'll only charge you five percent."

Amy figured out what she was going to owe and entered it on her business record sheet.

		$83.50
Withdraw from bank to pay for trip	$80.00	−80.00
		$ 3.50
Leave in bank to keep acct. open	$ 3.50	− 3.50
		$ 0.00
Loan from Mom	$35.00	
interest $35.00 × .05 (5%) =	$ 1.75	
	$36.75	−36.75
		−$36.75

"It looks as if my business is losing money," Amy said. "But when I come back from my trip I'll sell enough terrariums to start making profits again."

Two weeks later Amy came back from her camping trip sunburned and happy. "I had a terrific time!" she told Danny. "And I spent all my money, so I'd better get ready for the swap meet."

Danny looked worried. "I'm glad you had a good time," he said. "But I'm afraid I have some bad news for you. Some kind of bug got into your terrariums. A lot of the plants look pretty sick."

"Oh, no!" cried Amy. She raced out back to look at the damage. It looked as if every terrarium had been

"OH NO!" CRIED AMY. SHE RACED OUT BACK
TO LOOK AT THE DAMAGE.

invaded. "All these terrariums need some new plants
before I can sell them," she moaned.

Danny had followed her outside. "That's not your only
problem, Amy," he said. "I found out that the swap
meet moves inside for the winter. You need a new permit
and that's going to cost you five dollars."

"Now what am I going to do?" said Amy. She sat down on the steps to think things over.

Amy felt sure there were still plenty of customers for her terrariums. But she needed some money right away to get her business going again. "Since I haven't even started to pay back my first loan yet, I probably won't be able to get another one," she thought. "Maybe there's some other way to get new capital. I wonder if anyone would like to invest in my business?"

4
Investing–
A Piece of the Action

Investing in a business means buying a share in that business. Lots of businesses need investors to provide additional capital. When investors buy a share in a business, they are gambling that the business will be successful and that their shares will increase in value. Investing in a business is a risk; unlike a bank, a business does not guarantee a certain increase in the money invested. The business could do poorly and the investors' shares would decrease in value. On the other hand, if the business does well, the investors can make much more than they would by lending money to a bank.

Sometimes a business borrows money from a bank. But the business owner may not be able to borrow as much money as he needs. Also, when he borrows he must promise to pay back that money plus interest. If he can find investors, he will have to give up a share of his profits, but the investors' money will remain in the business. He doesn't have to pay it back to them as he

THE INVESTORS HAVE NOT LENT THEIR MONEY; THEY'VE BOUGHT PART OF THE BUSINESS.

does to the bank. The investors have not lent their money; they've bought part of the business.

Amy sat down to figure out what she needed to keep her terrarium business running. "If I replace the damaged plants in the 16 terrariums I have, I'll be able to sell those for a total of $48.00," she said to herself. "Then I can use $36.75 of that profit to repay my loan. But the problem is, I need money for the new plants and the permit before I can even sell those terrariums. And I'd like to get another batch of 25 terrariums ready to sell now, because I won't have time to do it after school starts."

Amy made a list of the money she needed.

EXPENSES

$ 5.00 permit
1.00 replace damaged plants
13.75 raw materials for 25 terrariums
$19.75

She realized that with $20 additional capital she could get her business moving again.

Amy called a meeting with Danny and Joan. She explained her problem and asked them if they wanted to invest $10.00 each in her business.

"What would I get for my $10.00?" Danny asked.

"For a $10.00 investment, I'm willing to give you a 20% share of the profits of my business," Amy replied.

Joan looked puzzled. "How much money will that be?"

Amy pulled out a sheet of paper. "Here's my estimate of how much money you'll make," she said.

INCOME	EXPENSES

SALES
16 × $3.00 = $ 48.00
25 × $3.00 = 75.00
$123.00
INVESTMENT $ 20.00
$143.00

	repay loan	$36.75
	replace plants	1.00
	swap meet permit	5.00
	raw materials	13.75
− 56.50		$56.50
$ 86.50		
	reinvestment in raw	
− 16.50	materials, etc.	$16.50
$ 70.00 profit		

$70.00
× .20 (20%)
―――――
$14.00 profit each for Danny and Joan

"Your 20% share of the profits will come to $14.00," said Amy.

"That's pretty good," Joan said. "I'll get back a lot more than I invested, and I'll still own 20% of the business. I think it's a terrific investment."

Danny was still looking at Amy's calculations. "Why don't I get 20% of $86.50?" he asked Amy. "I don't see why you subtracted $16.50 from the profits."

"Because to keep the business running, we have to spend some of the profits for more raw materials and other expenses," Amy explained. "I figured $16.50 is about what we'll need. If we don't spend it all, what's left over will be counted as profit."

"I get it," Danny said. "Sounds okay to me. Here's my $10.00."

"And mine too," said Joan. "I've never owned a share of a business before. This should be fun!"

5
Competition!

With the investment of Danny's and Joan's new capital, Amy's terrarium business was back on its feet. In a couple of weeks Amy had made enough money to pay back her loan.

"Here's the money I borrowed from you, Mom," she said, "plus 5% interest. Thanks for helping me out."

"You're a prompt payer, Amy," said her mother. "Your credit is always good with me."

After paying back the loan, Amy decided to figure out how her business was doing.

Amy's Terrariums Business Record Sheet

Danny and Joan's investment		$20.00
EXPENSES		
replace plants	$ 1.00	
swap meet permit	5.00	
	$ 6.00	— 6.00
		$14.00
SALES 6 × $3.00 = $18.00		+18.00
		$32.00
SALES 7 × $3.00 = $21.00		+21.00
		$53.00
EXPENSES		
repayment of loan	$36.75	
raw materials for 25		
terrariums	$13.75	—50.50
	$50.50	$ 2.50

"I sure don't have much profit right now," Amy said to herself, "but I've paid all my expenses. The money I get from selling the rest of the terrariums will be all profit."

As Amy was on her way out to work on some more terrariums, Joan came rushing in the door. "Oh, Amy," she gasped, "I have terrible news! Guess what I just saw on my way home from my violin lesson!"

"What?" asked Amy.

"That new gift shop on Main Street has a whole bunch of terrariums for sale, and they're the same price as ours!"

"Oh, no!" Amy exclaimed. "What do they look like?"

"They look a lot like ours," Joan said. "I think somebody stole our idea!"

"That sounds serious," said Amy. "We'd better call a meeting."

That evening the girls explained the problem to Danny. "So you see, we have competition," Amy finished. "This big company is selling the same thing at the same price."

"How can they do that?" asked Danny. "Don't they have a lot more expenses than we do?"

"Yes," said Joan. "Besides their rent and shipping and labor costs, a big company has to pay taxes."

Joan and Danny are right. A large business does have many more expenses than a person who works out of his or her home. A company usually must own or rent a factory, an office, and perhaps a store to sell its prod-

THAT EVENING THE GIRLS EXPLAINED THE PROBLEM
TO DANNY.

ucts. These buildings need heat, light, telephones, and usually machinery. A company must pay its employees and must pay for shipping its products and for mailing bills and catalogs.

In addition, companies, like individuals, must pay taxes. Tax money pays for the goods and services the government provides for the whole community. For example, highways, parks, buildings such as schools, libraries, and prisons, and war materials such as planes and bombs are goods that are bought by the government with tax money. Taxes also pay for services like fire and police protection, help for the sick and the needy, education, administering justice through the courts, and building and maintaining public property. The idea behind taxes is that because everyone uses or benefits from these goods and services, their cost is divided up among all the members of the community. Taxes are collected by the federal, state, and local governments. These taxes may be collected in various ways. People pay tax on the money they earn (income tax), on the land and buildings they own (property tax), and on the things they buy (sales tax). Businesses pay tax on these things too.

With all these expenses, doesn't a large company have to charge more for its product than an individual does? No, because the cost of producing each item is lower than when it is made by hand. A large business uses machinery to mass-produce its product, turning out many more than a person can in the same amount of time. And with machines doing the work, fewer employees are needed, which also cuts down on expenses.

Another way large businesses save money is by buying

their raw materials in very large quantities. For instance, the man who sells plants for terrariums is willing to charge less for each plant if he can sell a lot of them, all to one company. By doing this he saves the time and expense of moving the plants from place to place and taking care of them while he tries to find a whole lot of smaller customers. Since Amy can't use 1000 plants at one time, she can't take advantage of this lower price. The same holds true for the other raw materials. So even though a large company has to spend a lot of money to pay for all its expenses, it is actually spending less to produce each item.

"Well, I see we have a problem," said Amy. "That big company really can make terrariums just like ours and sell them for the same price."

"Besides, they probably sell their terrariums in a whole bunch of stores," Joan moaned. "And we only have our one stand at the swap meet."

Amy, Joan, and Danny sat thinking gloomy thoughts. How could they get people to come to the swap meet and buy their terrariums instead of buying the ones made by the big company?

Suddenly Danny said, "I've got it! We'll advertise!"

"But what are we going to advertise?" asked Amy.

"Our terrariums are the same price as theirs and they look an awful lot alike. What's different about ours?"

"You are!" exclaimed Danny.

"Me?" asked Amy in surprise.

"Sure," Joan chimed in. "You make them all yourself, by hand, and people want to know their plants come from a good home—they're healthy and you take good care of them."

"And don't forget, you were here first," Danny added. "We'll make a sign for the swap meet."

Buy the Original
AMY'S TERRARIUMS

"Yeah," said Amy. "And we'll put up a bunch of signs all over town telling people my terrariums are hand-made."

"We need a slogan," Joan said. "How about 'Planted with loving fingers'?"

"Great," said Danny.

Amy looked worried. "Wait a minute. It will cost money to advertise, and right now we only have $2.50 in cash."

"We can do a lot of advertising for $2.50," said Danny.

"WE CAN DO A LOT OF ADVERTISING
FOR $2.50," SAID DANNY.

"It's a risk," Joan admitted, "but it's worth doing if it
attracts more customers."

"Okay," said Amy. "Let's get these loving fingers to
work!"

6
Inflation Strikes!

The advertising campaign was a big success. After spending their $2.50 on green paper and white paint, Amy and Joan and Danny covered the town with posters. At the next swap meet they sold 18 of the 28 terrariums they had brought.

"Wow! What a fantastic day!" exclaimed Joan.

"I've never sold so many in one day!" Amy said. "Our advertising really paid off."

But the next week they only sold 7 of the remaining 10 terrariums. Many people stopped to admire Amy's terrariums, but most of them said they already had one at home.

"It seems as if there's not much demand for terrariums anymore," Amy told Joan and Danny. "I'm not sure I should make any more."

Joan thought it over. "Well, they aren't selling as fast as they were, but with school and homework you won't be able to make them as fast either. And by the time you've made another 25, people will be starting to think about Christmas presents. The demand will probably increase again."

"I agree," said Danny. "Even with a slow day, look how well we're doing."

Amy's Terrariums Business Record Sheet

		$ 2.50
EXPENSES		
advertising materials	$2.50	— 2.50
		$ 0.00
SALES 18 × $3.00 = $54.00		+54.00
		$54.00
SALES 7 × $3.00 = $21.00		+21.00
		$75.00

"Great!" Joan exclaimed. "Even after we take out the money for more raw materials, we'll all be making a good profit."

"Okay," said Amy. "We'd better reinvest right now."

But the next day Amy called an emergency meeting. "We've got big problems," she told the others.

Amy explained that when she went to the pet store, the cheap fishbowls were all gone. Mr. Buckley told her he could order more, but the price would have to go up.

"He told me he hadn't made any profit on the twenty-five-cent ones—he sold them cheap just to get rid of them. But now he has to pay more for them himself, and he sells them for 75¢. He said since I want to buy 25 of them, I could have them for 65¢ apiece."

"But that's more than twice as much as before!" Danny exclaimed.

"I know," replied Amy. "And that's not all. Remember how cold it was last week? The plant man lost a lot of plants and he had to move the others indoors. He's having trouble getting more plants right now, so his prices have gone up too. We'll have to pay $10.00 for the plants we need."

"That's terrible," Joan said. "What will that do to our profits?"

"Let's figure it out," said Danny.

SALES   EXPENSES

$25 \times \$3.00 = \$75.00$

fishbowls $(25 \times \$.65)$	$16.25
plants	10.00
soil, etc.	2.50
	$28.75

$$-28.75$$
$$\$46.25$$

20% share: $\$46.25 \times .20 = \$\ 9.25$ for Danny
20% share: $\$46.25 \times .20 = \$\ 9.25$ for Joan
60% share: $\$46.25 \times .60 = \$27.75$ for Amy

"Well, we'll still be making money," said Joan, "but not as much as before."

"I have an idea," Danny said. "Since our suppliers raised their prices, why don't we raise ours? Then we'll be able to make the same profit."

"We can't do that," Amy said. "If our prices are higher than the big terrarium company's prices, no one will buy our terrariums. And the big company probably won't need to raise its prices—at least, not right away. They can buy their supplies more cheaply than we can, and besides, they probably have a lot of terrariums in stock, ready to sell."

"I guess you're right," Danny replied. "We can't stay

in business if we raise our prices. But our costs have gone up. It seems as if our money isn't worth as much as it used to be."

Amy's business is experiencing a common problem. It is called inflation. Inflation means that prices of most things are going up. It is a problem because prices and income usually don't go up at the same rate. Suppose you earned $100 in 1970 and you bought a bicycle for $25. This means you spent 25% of your income on a bicycle. But what if prices have doubled by 1979? If you earn the same amout ($100) in 1979 but you have to pay $50 for the same kind of bicycle, you are spending 50% of your income for the same goods. The $100 you have in 1979 is worth only half as much as the $100 you had in 1970.

1970	1979
$100 buys 4 bicycles	$100 buys 2 bicycles

You can see that you would need to earn $200 in 1979 to buy the same things you could buy with $100 in 1970.

This means that the value of money is not fixed. It goes up or down, depending on how much you can buy

THE $100 YOU HAVE IN 1979 IS WORTH ONLY HALF AS MUCH AS THE $100 YOU HAD IN 1970.

with a certain amount of money at any given time. So the "real" value of a dollar may be less today than it was a year ago—a dollar is only worth what you can buy with it.

Inflation is a very serious problem for the whole country. The government tries to slow down inflation by controlling the ways money is circulated through the economy. But so far these controls have not had much success in lowering the rate of inflation. As our society grows more complex, it becomes more difficult to understand all the various factors that affect the economy.

7
To Greener Pastures

Amy had been thinking about the future of her terrarium business.

"The way I see it," she said to Joan and Danny, "we have several problems. First of all, our costs are going up and we can't raise our prices because of competition. So we're going to be making a much smaller profit.

"Also, it looks as if the demand for terrariums is going down. Pretty soon everyone in town who wants one will have a terrarium. When that happens, the big company can sell terrariums in other towns, but we won't be able to do that.

"And another problem is that I don't have much free time anymore. Because of school and swim team practice, it will take me a month to make as many terrariums as I made in a week this summer. My time is more valuable now because I have so many other things to spend it on, but I'm going to be getting paid less for the time I spend on terrariums.

"The last thing is that we don't know for sure that the demand for terrariums will go up even at Christmas. What if we make all these terrariums and then we can't sell them?

"All in all, I wonder if investing so much of our profits and my time when we're not very sure of our market isn't too much of a risk."

Joan and Danny looked at each other. Then they turned to Amy. "You mean we should go out of business?" asked Joan.

"But, Amy," said Danny, "it's your business. Won't you be upset if you have to close it down?"

"No," replied Amy. "I've done what I wanted to do. I paid for the camping trip, I repaid my loan, and I've made a pretty good profit. I think it's time to declare ourselves out of business and divide up the $75.00 profit."

$75.00 × .20 = $15.00 Joan's share
$75.00 × .20 = $15.00 Danny's share
$75.00 × .60 = $45.00 Amy's share

"Well, I'm satisfied," said Joan. "I put in ten dollars and I got fifteen dollars back. That's a pretty good investment."

"Okay with me," Danny said. "But don't forget, we still have three terrariums."

"That's easy," Amy laughed. "We'll each keep one."

When the money and the terrariums had been divided up, Joan looked a little sad. "It was fun to be in business. I'm sorry it's over," she said.

"There's no reason why we can't start up another business," Amy told her. "Now that we all have some money, we can form a partnership. We'll invest an equal amount of capital and we'll each do an equal amount of the work. Then we'll split the profits equally three ways."

"Great!" said Danny. "But what kind of business will it be?"

"Let's think of something there's a big demand for," Joan said. "How about—"

"I've got it!" Danny interrupted. "We could make—"

Amy broke in. "I know what we'll do. Everyone wants a—"

Index

DATE DUE

FEB 12			
MAR 5			
MAR 19			
MAR 28			
MAR 27			
NOV 7			
FEB 27			
MAY 11			
APR 4			
APR 16			
FEB 12 1997			
SEP 23			

GAYLORD PRINTED IN U.S.A.